① **Rome, 121:** Birth of Marcus.

② **Naples, 143:** Visits as a teenager on a trip with family.

③ **Canusium, 162:** Visits Lucis Verus while he is ill.

④ **Carnuntum, 171:** Sets up base of operations for First Marcomannic War. Returns in 178 to fight once more.

⑤ **Aquincum (now Budapest), 173:** Marcus writes a portion of the *Meditations*.

⑥ **Tarsus, 175:** Meets the young Greek rhetorician Hermogenes.

⑦ **Alexandria, 176:** Visits following defeat of Avidius Cassius.

⑧ **Smyrna, 176:** Touring empire, meets with philosophy students.

⑨ **Athens, 176:** Sets up chairs in philosophy and is initiated into the Eleusinian mysteries.

⑩ **Vindobona (now Vienna), 180:** Death.

A s i a
M i n o r

⑧ SMYRNA

HALALA •

TARSUS ⑥

EAN SEA

⑦
ALEXANDRIA

Egypt

N
NE
E
SE
S
SW
W
NW

THE BOY WHO WOULD BE KING

Make Marcus proud

BY RYAN HOLIDAY

THE PAINTED PORCH BOOKSHOP

SECOND EDITION

ISBN: 978-0-578-81004-1 (print)

10 9 8 7 6 5 4 3 2

"If, at some point in your life,
you should come across anything better than
justice, wisdom, discipline, courage—
it must be an extraordinary thing indeed."

MARCUS AURELIUS, *MEDITATIONS*

You might think that every
little boy should like
to be king.

But
Marcus
Aurelius
didn't.

"Why me?"
was all
he could
think.

"The gods choose things for us,"
his mother said.

"All we can choose is how we respond."

"It seems
very hard,"
he said.

"To whom much is given, much is expected," she told him.

When the sun rose the next day, it found
Marcus laying in bed. That's where his
teacher Rusticus found him too.

Is this what you were put on this earth to do?"
he asked. "To hide under the warm covers?"

Marcus had
gone to school,
but now
his education
truly began.

"Your path will not be an easy one,"
Rusticus told him,
"but I can show you the way."

Into the boy's hands,
he placed a book.

Then another

and another

and another.

"What does reading books
have to do with
being a king?"
Marcus asked.

"Everything," Rusticus answered.

"Through the pages of a book," Rusticus said, "we can talk to people who lived long ago, and learn easily what they learned with great difficulty."

When Marcus finished reading,
he assumed he knew everything
there was to know.

"Life's lessons only begin
with books," Rusticus said.
"They don't stop there."

Together, they watched
officials give speeches.

They spoke
with wise elders.

Like a true Roman,
Marcus learned
to ride and to hunt . . .

. . . and to wrestle.

"It's not fair," Marcus said,
after losing to his brother one day.
"Lucius is so much stronger than me."

"How do you think
I got that way?"
Lucius said.

"It's alright, Marcus," Rusticus said. "Nothing should encourage us as much as the different qualities of the people around us."

"One person's modesty . . .

. . . another's
cheerfulness.

someone's beauty . . .

. . . someone's work ethic."

"We can learn from everyone," Rusticus said.

"Our opponents, our friends, everyone is better than us at something."

"But look at that kid," Marcus yelled.
"He's cheating!"

"Even there we can learn how *not* to be,"
Rusticus replied.

"And the way to beat a cheater
is to not be like them."

There were lessons every day,
and sometimes Marcus felt sorry for himself.

Lucius felt sorry for himself, too.

"Why was Marcus picked instead of me?" Lucius wondered.

"I didn't ask for any of this," Marcus grumbled.

"Never let yourself
be heard complaining,"
their mother told them,
"not even to yourselves."

You might think that
a future king can do
anything he wants.

But no one is fit
to rule who hasn't
first mastered
themselves.

"Moderation in all things,"
Rusticus told Marcus,
"and remember,
some things not at all."

Still, sometimes mischief fluttered
in Marcus's little heart.

Like the time he played a prank on the
shepherd, scattering his sheep in all directions.

His mother was most disappointed.

"To whom much is given, much is expected,"
she said again. "To do wrong to one person
is to do wrong to yourself."

Marcus decided he had to see
the kingdom he was supposed to lead.

So he walked the busy streets of Rome,
where there were
hungry beggars
and desperate
gladiators . . .

. . . scheming senators
and
aggressive merchants . . .

. . . where the rich lived well
and
the poor suffered.

It was too much.

So he ran away to his family's home
in the countryside, where he could be alone,
without anyone or anything to bother him.

He could walk through the fields of wheat
bending low under their own weight . . .

. . . pick the ripe olives
from the trees . . .

... watch the boars run
with flecks of foam
on their mouths ...

. . . and sit at the top of a hill
and look down on Rome,
protected from
everything he didn't like.

"You know, this isn't what you were put here for either," Rusticus said when he found Marcus.

"It's not right to ignore what you know is not right. There is no good in all this training if you don't use it. We've spent so much time talking about what a good king is like. Soon you'll have to *be one*."

"What if I am not ready?
What if I'm not
smart enough?
What if I mess up?"

"Just do your best, step by step," Rusticus said. "That's no small thing."

That night Marcus had a dream
that his shoulders were made of ivory.

On them
rested the
purple
cloak of the
emperor.

When he awoke early the next morning,
Marcus knew it was time.

It was his turn to make decisions,
to carry the load . . .

... and to thank Rusticus the best
way there is to thank a teacher,
by living up to what they taught us.

So Marcus sold the palace
jewels to feed the poor.

He gave the gladiators wooden swords
so they could not get hurt in the arena.

He upheld the laws,
lived by them,
and insisted that
everyone do
the same.

When he felt that he might lose his temper, he counted all the letters of the alphabet before he said anything.

And then he surprised everyone

by naming his brother, Lucius, *co-emperor.*

"It doesn't matter if you're tired or well-rested.
It doesn't matter if it's hard or easy.
If you're cold or warm.

What counts, whether you're a kid or a king or anything in between," Marcus said, "is that you do the right thing."

You might think this all made
Marcus Aurelius very popular . . .

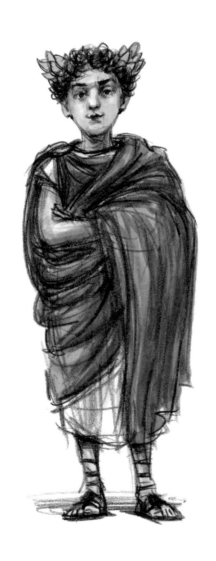

. . . and you are right.

They built
statues of him
and threw parades.

Crowds cheered as he passed.

It was nice,
but of course,
not why he did it.

"At first, I thought I was unlucky that this happened to me," Marcus said.

"But now I see that it was a gift."

"The job of emperor was a gift," Rusticus and his mother said, "because you made it one."

Marcus Aurelius lived long, long ago.

And the gods have chosen many
boys and girls to rule since.
But Marcus's example
stands eternal.

Courage.

Justice.

Discipline.

Wisdom.

An extraordinary thing indeed.

THE END.

AFTERWORD

The real Marcus Aurelius was just a boy when the emperor Hadrian noticed something in him. Without an heir to the throne, Hadrian made the incredible decision to groom Marcus to be the ruler of the world.

From what we know, Marcus Aurelius was already bright, serious, and honest at an early age. But it was the influence of his stepfather(s), Hadrian and Antoninus, as well as his philosophy tutors—who included not only Rusticus but also Sextus and Fronto—that really shaped him. To be a king is not a job that anyone can truly prepare for, but Marcus had the best teachers and role models that a person could ask for.

In this story, we have combined characters and compressed quotes to illustrate the impact that philosophy is supposed to have on a person: it's supposed to make you better. Make you kinder, smarter, stronger, fairer, and more just.

For a lot of people, power corrupts. For Marcus Aurelius, it made him better. Why was that? The only answer is Stoicism.

"It stares you in the face," he wrote to himself in his *Meditations*. "No role is so well suited to philosophy as the one you happen to be in right now."

As a philosophy, Stoicism is built around the four virtues we've talked about in these pages: Courage. Discipline. Justice. Wisdom.

Those were the virtues that Marcus lived by. There is not enough room to list his accomplishments as a leader, but they were many:

- He guided Rome through a devastating pandemic (selling off the palace furnishings to keep the country out of debt)

- He shared power with his brother (a feat no king before or since managed)

- He passed legislation protecting Rome's most vulnerable (including its slaves and gladiators)

- He led the Roman army in battle when its borders were invaded

- He peacefully dealt with civil unrest and an attempted coup

- He wrote a short book called *Meditations* (which inspired much of the thinking in the book you've just read)

The story of Marcus Aurelius is the story of all of us.

Destiny selects each person for something.

Will we choose to accept it? Will we become the person we're meant to be? That is the question.

My hope is that whoever you are, whatever your age, this book will begin a journey for you not unlike Marcus's. One that makes you better, that challenges you, that has a real impact on the world.

It's worth noting that Marcus Aurelius kept at his studies long after he became king. Not only did he keep Rusticus with him, greeting him with a kiss each time he saw him and always asking for advice, but he kept reading and asking questions as long as he lived. We are told one story about Marcus, toward the end of his life.

A friend spotted the emperor leaving the palace. Where are you going, my lord, he asked? "To see Sextus the philosopher," Marcus replies, "to learn that which I do not yet know." Even as an old man, Marcus was still gathering his tablets and going to school.

Whether you're a kid or a king or anything in between, that's the model for us to follow. That's what destiny calls us to do.

Keep reading. Keep learning.

Courage. Discipline. Justice. Wisdom.

It's an extraordinary thing indeed.

ACKNOWLEDGMENTS

This work would not be possible without the wonderful translations and work of many translators, scholars and historians over the years. We thank them—especially Gregory Hays, Stephen Hanselman, Donald Robertson, Marguerite Yourcenar, Frank Lynn and Ernest Renan. We also owe a debt of gratitude to Shawn Coyne for pairing us together, Nils Parker for his edits and inputs, Milt Deherrera for managing it, Rebecca DeField for creating the map, and Lorie DeWorken for putting the package together.

RYAN: This was a book title I had floating in my head for some time but it was my son Clark who brought it to life for me. I'm so glad to have received his wonderful contributions, his edits and all the bedtimes he let me use to create it. My wife Samantha was a guiding voice, as always. In the eight months that this book evolved during the pandemic, I watched my younger son, Jones, go from a baby to a toddler who could sit and read it with us. In that way, we are, as Marcus said, *fortunate that this happened to us.*

VICTOR: Serious gratitude to Ryan, Nils, and Shawn. We artists live for these projects and they don't happen often. This one is for the grandkids.

ABOUT THE AUTHOR

Ryan Holiday is one of the world's foremost writers on ancient philosophy and its place in everyday life. His books like *The Obstacle Is The Way*, *Ego Is the Enemy*, *The Daily Stoic*, and the #1 *New York Times* bestseller *Stillness Is the Key* have sold millions of copies worldwide and been translated into over 30 languages. He lives outside Austin, Texas, with his wife and two boys... and cows and donkeys and goats.

ABOUT THE ILLUSTRATOR

Victor Juhasz straddles both humorous and serious illustration and appears in many major publications. Among the books he's illustrated are *D is for Democracy: A Citizen's Alphabet*, *G is for Gladiator*, and *R is for Rhyme*. He lives with his wife in the New York Berkshires.

MORE BOOKS
BY RYAN HOLIDAY

The Daily Stoic: 366 Meditations on
Wisdom, Perseverance, and the Art of Living

The Daily Stoic Journal: 366 Days of
Writing and Reflection on the Art of Living

Lives of the Stoics: The Art of Living
from Zeno to Marcus Aurelius

The Obstacle Is the Way:
The Timeless Art of Turning Trials into Triumph

Ego Is the Enemy

Stillness Is the Key

For a daily Stoic-inspired meditation,
sign up at **DailyStoic.com/email**.

And listen along with the Daily Stoic podcast.